BFI FILM CLASS
. . . .
Edward Buscom
SERIES EDIT

Colin MacCabe and David Meeker
SERIES CONSULTANTS

Cinema is a fragile medium. Many of the great classic films of the past now exist, if at all, in damaged or incomplete prints. Concerned about the deterioration in the physical state of our film heritage, the National Film and Television Archive, a Division of the British Film Institute, has compiled a list of 360 key films in the history of the cinema. The long-term goal of the Archive is to build a collection of perfect show-prints of these films, which will then be screened regularly at the Museum of the Moving Image in London in a year-round repertory.

BFI Film Classics is a series of books commissioned to stand alongside these titles. Authors, including film critics and scholars, film-makers, novelists, historians and those distinguished in the arts, have been invited to write on a film of their choice, drawn from the Archive's list. Each volume presents the author's own insights into the chosen film, together with a brief production history and a detailed filmography, notes and bibliography. The numerous illustrations have been specially made from the Archive's own prints.

With new titles published each year, the BFI Film Classics series will rapidly grow into an authoritative and highly readable guide to the great films of world cinema.

Could scarcely be improved upon ... informative, intelligent, jargon-free companions.
The Observer

Cannily but elegantly packaged BFI Classics will make for a neat addition to the most discerning shelves.
New Statesman & Society

THE FLESH...
So Weak!

THE SPIRIT...
So Willing!

GENE TIERNEY
with that taunt in her smile

REX HARRISON
with that haunt in his kiss
and

GEORGE SANDERS
without a ghost of a chance

The
Ghost and
Mrs. Muir

The delectable best-seller becomes the delight of your life on the screen!

with
EDNA BEST

20th CENTURY-FOX TRIUMPH!

VANESSA BROWN · Anna Lee · Robert Coote · Natalie Wood · Isobel Elsom · Victoria Horne

Directed by JOSEPH L. MANKIEWICZ · Produced by FRED KOHLMAR

Screen Play by Philip Dunne · From the Novel by R. A. Dick

SIGNATURE

BFI FILM CLASSICS

THE GHOST AND MRS MUIR

....

Frieda Grafe

BRITISH FILM INSTITUTE

bfi

BFI PUBLISHING

First published in 1995 by the
BRITISH FILM INSTITUTE
21 Stephen Street, London W1P 2LN

The British Film Institute exists
to promote appreciation, enjoyment, protection and
development of moving image culture in and throughout
the whole of the United Kingdom.
Its activities include the National Film and
Television Archive; the National Film Theatre;
the Museum of the Moving Image;
the London Film Festival; the production and
distribution of film and video; funding and support for
regional activities; Library and Information Services;
Stills, Posters and Designs; Research;
Publishing and Education; and the monthly
Sight and Sound magazine.

British Library Cataloguing in Publication Data
A catalogue record for this book is available from the British Library

ISBN 0–85170–484–0

Stills courtesy of Twentieth Century-Fox Film Company

Designed by
Andrew Barron & Collis Clements Associates

Typesetting by
Fakenham Photosetting Limited, Norfolk

Printed in Great Britain by
The Trinity Press, Worcester

CONTENTS

· ·

Thanks
David Meeker
Janet Bergstrom
Michael Friend
Enno Patalas

When a woman writes a book . . .

IN THE NAME OF THE AUTHOR

. . . .

When a woman writes a book. Where that leads. Backwards, at any rate, and to an awareness of how interlaced things are, and how much of one's self derives from others.

'What they didn't know about life would fill an encyclopaedia,' it says in the novel on which the film was based. Fortunately we have books as a guide. The voice that dictates Mrs Muir's first and only book belongs to a dead captain, who is supposed to have committed suicide. She knows otherwise, once she has glanced at his portrait. She has built her nest in his house by the sea, having fled there from London to escape her dependence on her inlaws. She is a parasite, a stubborn one, in every respect. This is how she finds herself. She turns a strange and uncanny place into her home and defies a ghost.

She is a naive author, and so smart. A term relating to sexual intercourse need only come into her head, and she immediately takes it as proof of the real existence of the captain: she would never have described it so bluntly!

'She turns a strange and uncanny place into her home'

9

Where are we supposed to think her knowledge comes from? From the books she read as a young girl in her father's library, of course. She went straight from there into marriage to an architect, who was in fact supposed to rebuild her father's library.

....

In 1945 Fox bought the film rights to the novel *The Ghost and Mrs Muir*, which had been published in Britain – whereby a completed work was changed back into material. The author's rights were forfeited by the sale. The author's son complained that his mother didn't get a penny for the family television series based on the film in the 1960s.

Philip Dunne wrote – alone, he says – the script that represents his reading of the novel. Its adaptation for the cinema has the advantage of honesty. There is no common denominator between cinematic images and the novelistic imagination, but quite definitely a difference between the description of what is heard and the depiction of what is seen. Mankiewicz, usually famous as a rewriter who compulsively had to leave his mark on everything that passed through his hands, denies all paternity. His statements about the film are sparse and monosyllabic: a piece of hack-work, taken on purely out of expedience. The film was supposed to prove that he had what it takes to be a dependable studio director. In other words, to be an executive employee on a smoothly running production line, who knew how to turn an assigned script and assigned actors into a film in a given time.

At almost the same time as the film was being made, Mankiewicz wrote an article for the bulletin of the Screen Writers' Guild – an association for the protection of authors' rights of which he was a co-founder – in which he explained his conception of what a film writer was. For him the root of all evil lies in the fact that the screenplay is written by one person and the film is shot by another. While, because of a lack of experience with the technical side of film production, he happily accepted a division of labour in which his cameraman made the pictures and he paid most of his attention to the actors, Mankiewicz nevertheless believed that a single person should be responsible for screenplay and direction. Separating them led to monstrosity. And to prostitution – and he always describes himself as a willing victim. He likes to criticise himself in terms normally reserved for the opposite sex: 'the oldest whore on the beat'.

The film-conscious screenwriter writes his script in such a way that it contains within itself the principles of its realisation, and the filming is only the second part of the process: 'Film-writing and directing are two components of the unit that is guaranteed by the person of the screenwriter.' He wanted to direct, not so much because he wished to keep control of the filming of his own screenplays as because he saw in film-writing a possibility for his medium – not the only one – which had not yet been tested, and one which was held in some contempt.

The Ghost and Mrs Muir conforms to the Hollywood system, and is anything but an *auteur* film. According to Dunne, Mankiewicz contributed only some passages of dialogue. They are so ostentatiously witty that we hear the author talking rather than the characters themselves. As a scriptwriter he would have done things differently, and stressed different aspects, Mankiewicz explained in an interview published in *Cahiers du Cinéma*. But even this lack of intervention makes *The Ghost and Mrs Muir* a true Mankiewicz film – if we are prepared to accept Godard's definition, expressed as a twenty-year-old: 'His films are like missed rendezvous.'

It was just a love story, Mankiewicz continued in that same interview: 'You've got the wind, you've got the sea, you've got the search for something else. And the disappointments you encounter. Those are the feelings I always wanted to get across, and I think you can find traces of them in almost all my films.'

Something of Mankiewicz's spirit must have found its way into the film independently of his intentions, something foreign which, in retrospect, seems very much his own. Seen from the *auteur* perspective, regardless of whether it is Mankiewicz's idea or a construction on the part of the viewer familiar with his work, the film gains an extra dimension. As if by chance, and rather spookily, it already contains the elements which later, in a more developed form, characterise his films. But when the film was made he must have been blind.

He is thinking in terms of credits, whereas the material is throwing up *auteur* questions in which he has a consuming interest. He sees a love story whereas the problem is the relation between the sexes and the androgyny of ideas. A theme for a sound film is handed to him on a plate: language less as expression than as a driving force. Language as a mask, as a convention, something that runs away with the speaker, revealing that it constitutes his very depths. Language is the true source of pleasure in the film; identification and verisimilitude are secondary. He is also given a time structure, the ideal flashback, of which he had always dreamed, not just a narrative trick, but the present and the past folded into one – but he thinks he's making genre cinema, a formula picture! And he, the famous *homme à femmes*, who so prided himself on being such an excellent connoisseur and confidant of women, missed the opportunity to film a woman's story intimately, from a woman's point of view.

Think of the wonderful life we could have had together, whispers the captain's voice to the sleeping Lucy. And the wonderful film that Mankiewicz could have made, the one that begins to take shape in our minds when we read what he had to say: 'Men are made up, for the most part, of large, predictable, conforming elements. Men react as they are taught to react. Women are, in comparison, as if assembled by the wind. They're made up of and react to tiny impulses. Inflections, colours, sounds. They hear things men cannot.'

It isn't in the spirit of the novel when, in the film, the captain, the ghost, takes his leave of the sleeping Mrs Muir with the words: 'Lucia, my dear, you wrote the book, you and no one else.' The novel leaves open the question of intellectual rights. Nor do the initials in front of the author's surname deliver any clues as to gender. R. A. Dick was a pseudonym. Josephine Aimée Campbell Leslie published her first novel in 1945, at the age of forty-seven. The initials were taken from her father, Robert Abercromby. He was a sea captain by profession. She always wanted to look different, Lucy confesses to the captain in the novel, to have 'an aristocratic Roman nose like my father's.'

Not that this anonymous little studio film could rise in value just because life in the shape of the author's own history had fed into it. But it is as if a work started under a false name had automatically generated additional pseudonyms, as if a loosening of firm connections were spreading in all directions, as if doubts as to attribution were extending through language to include the images themselves, and calling their origin into question. The atmosphere competes with the directness of the images, and condenses into forms that correspond to the vocabulary of Mrs Muir and her Cockney cook, which drifts off into seaman's slang and unlady-like cursing: 'Blast your eyes!'

Mrs Muir's seaman's yarn is published as a book by an

anonymous author. In her search for a publisher she encounters another writer publishing under a pseudonym. With his help she manages to place her book, when he gives her his appointment with a publisher. She only achieves access as a substitute for him. This other author is a cynical character who is repelled by children, but who writes successful children's books under the name of Uncle Neddy, 'the most awful trash', says his publisher, who makes money out of it. In the film the writer also paints in his free time. Under the name of Renoir, he jokes. And does he do anything under his own name, Miles Fairley, Mrs Muir wants to know. All he does then is play the fool, is Fairley's reply.

One of Mankiewicz's recurring criticisms of Hollywood is of the infantile scripts and the claim of those who make the decisions that, for the sake of business, you have to stick to the level of the adolescent audience; for the sake of business – in Mankiewicz's opinion the bosses effortlessly and naturally fall below even that level.

Miles Fairley is a compulsive skirt-chaser, whom Mrs Muir was taken in by, but in the book remembers in later years without a trace of shame. She won't allow anyone to take away what he means to her. Her affection is the expression of the self-confidence that writing has given her. He was the man of her dreams. 'You were in love with a man that never existed, because he did exist in your mind and in your heart,' the captain tells her. The film uses these lines from the book, but the captain uses them to refer to himself.

What Mrs Muir turns upside down in the book and the film is the acknowledged order according to which experience must come before books, and life must come before invention. She imagines herself into the painting of a man, and makes her story out of that. Out of the frame steps a blusterer, 'a booming foghorn of a man', who mainly comes out with prejudices and stereotypes about femininity and masculinity, about 'reasonable men and foolish women', who needs a woman's secretarial skills to put the unvarnished story of his life into a communicable linguistic form. He himself is not fully a master of English grammar.

This yields a headless text, with which the author does the deal of a lifetime and buys her way into a strange house.

Freedom from overly fixed positions, an amused mobility of points of view, has spilled into the film from the novel. It opens the door to all kinds of fantasies on the part of the viewer.

DIRECTOR'S STUDIO OF A CREATIVE PRODUCER
....

Darryl F. Zanuck ran 20th Century-Fox as a one-man show. He decided on the material, gave his blessing to the scripts – it was usually only then, in a kind of directorial typecasting, that the director was engaged – and after continuous viewing of the rushes he decided the final edit. His opponents and enemies too, such as Mankiewicz, valued his criticisms of the scripts and praised his abilities in the cutting room. John Ford even left the editing entirely up to him, he says. Which didn't mean much where Ford's films were concerned. Preminger also explained his preference for long takes by saying that they made it more difficult for Zanuck to interfere.

When Mankiewicz left MGM after an argument with Louis B. Mayer, who had only allowed him to serve as a producer, he was taken on by Joe Schenck's Fox with the best contract of his life, which, apart from a pay rise, gave him 'the right to stipulate on every property I undertook whether I wrote and/or directed and/or produced. I could do all or but one, at my choice.' At that time Zanuck was on war service in Europe.

The conflicts between these two very different, ambitious men were inevitable. The limited ground they had in common was the fact that they were both Hollywood agents through and through, with a love of the mass medium and the demands it made. Apart from that, they both wanted to use the script to escape Hollywood's tired film formulae and make films for grown-ups. They both wanted to make the audience think, one with fast editing, the other with long speeches. Zanuck thought highly of Mankiewicz as a writer of dialogue.

At the beginning of their collaboration, when *The Ghost and Mrs Muir* was made, Mankiewicz was chiefly concerned with learning how to stage a film on set, and for him that had less to do with the technical side of directing than it did with working with the actors. The mere fact that in the film he cast actors whom he also used subsequently, the complex diversity of voices and tones, shows that here he is already well on the way to his later films.

The choice of Gene Tierney for the role of Lucy Muir was a compromise, a recourse to what was available. Fox had no big stars. Zanuck's actresses were a stable of young girls, most of them with a past as cover-girls. If stars were needed, they had to be borrowed.

Norma Shearer and Claudette Colbert were discussed. Zanuck also thought of Olivia de Havilland and Katharine Hepburn. When the film came out, people laughed at Tierney's stilted British accent. To many people, her beauty is now the film's main attraction.

With Claudette Colbert in the part of Mrs Muir, it would have been easy for Mankiewicz to hit the risqué tone of the sophisticated comedy that he admired in Lubitsch, whom he took as a model. The surreal would thus have been given aesthetic sanction as lunacy. With Tierney, the rushes of the first few days' filming looked merely burlesque, to Philip Dunne's dismay. As Mankiewicz insisted on his approach, the matter was brought before Zanuck who, as Dunne had expected, supported the script and decided to start all over again following Dunne's conception, and to show Mrs Muir as 'a straightforward and practical woman who takes no nonsense from the ghost'.

At an earlier stage Zanuck had declared himself very pleased with the script and, by way of a small suggestion, had asked for a realistic treatment of the appearances of the ghost, of the illusion, as he put it,

Gene Tierney as Lucy Muir

1 6 'All you see is an illusion, like a blasted lantern slide'

with no tricks and wobbly dissolves, the quotation marks for the supernatural in the cinema: 'The audience starts to wonder about the technical trick and they forget the emotions of the moment.' They had just had a good experience – supported by good box-office receipts – with the Fox film *Sentimental Journey*, in which the audience accepted the straightforward visualisation of daydreams without further ado.

Zanuck's instructions speak for themselves. They are not prompted by a progressive idea of psychic reality, which the cinema's ghostly images of reality are so well able to grasp. The ghost was not to turn up as a frightening spook, but as a male dream-being. The imagination is rationalised by cinematic technique. The combination draws the viewer into the invention with greater intensity than fictions that try to present themselves as pure reality. It works if the viewer is willing to participate, and the ugly business of verisimilitude becomes an irrelevance.

The characters reflect on the events on screen:

CAPTAIN: All you see is an illusion, like a blasted lantern slide.
LUCY: It's not very convincing, but I suppose it's all right.

'To my knowledge,' a French critic wrote in 1950, in the *Gazette du Cinéma* (the article, signed E.S., is not, as is often supposed, by Eric Rohmer, who was an editor of the magazine but who cannot remember the name of the writer), '*The Ghost and Mrs Muir* is the only ghost film not to have *believed* in ghosts, the possibility of their existence, not even from the point of view of dramatic interest. In *The Ghost and Mrs Muir* the nature of the phantom is something precise ... "A ghost is the fear that one has of it." The fear or the desire.'

Captain Gregg is a good poltergeist because he is a creature of Mrs Muir's desires. Their cohabitation and its fruits, a book that they have written together, have the charm of a naive transgression, and are no less liberating for that.

No sex. Something utterly taboo in Hollywood films, and punished by the censors, is in this case a positive, plot-making precondition: Mrs Muir's avowed desire, which cannot be interpreted as a process of repression or inhibition. Even the attractions of erotically charged objects – the telescope in the bedroom, which the director turns into an object of cultlike devotion, a golden calf around which the camera dances – remain for that very reason harmless, and so don't create a risqué double standard, even if the Legion of Decency classified the film as 'morally objectionable in part for all'. Undoubtedly, there is ambiguity. There are, however, more archaic reasons for the irreconcilability of two people who are fond of each other but who inhabit different spheres. These give rise to projections. As the masculine is crossed with the feminine, and as the two poles are constantly switching sides, movement becomes transgression.

We do not believe, either, in projections; they are a genuine energy rather than an evasion. They take on solidity through their fixed, assumed context.

On this point at least, Zanuck and his director were in agreement, despite Mankiewicz's liking for things European and despite his Germanic inheritance of belief in culture: they were both set on making a resolutely American cinema. Harry Dawes in *The Barefoot Contessa* is the prototype American director, put together from 'a number of directors I have known, real Hollywood men like Gregory La Cava, Howard Hawks, Eddie Sutherland, William Wellman, who had the American eye, the cynical eye.' For Mankiewicz, *Citizen Kane* and *The Great McGinty* were exemplary American scripts.

Gene Tierney with Edna Best

Zanuck, who never let a commercially successful fashion go by – and ghost stories were in vogue in the 40s – wanted his ghost story to be played cool, in the Fox style. If there had to be any psychology, then let it be objective and American, a case to be cleared up, as in *Laura*: a slow-witted detective carried away by a painting of a woman who is supposed to be dead.

Conspicuous technical and theatrical effects confuse the audience and jeopardise the realistic transparency that Hollywood saw as its greatest quality: to behave as though this is how it was. The author, if there is one, must stay concealed. The outwardly conventional portrayal of *The Ghost and Mrs Muir*, a product of the studio apparatus and skilled technicians, is there to maintain the form. The film is transfigured by its subject, which Mankiewicz describes as mysterious. In order to understand it, he said, Gene Tierney needed the professional imagination of Rex Harrison and Edna Best – which can only mean what the actors, using their voices and gestures, are able to make of words and with words and then put on the screen.

Mankiewicz supported the movement carried by language with a great deal of camera movement, which discreetly links up with the restlessness of nature by the sea and the music of Bernard Herrmann. Mankiewicz says he was 'boom crazy' at the time – which caused Zanuck to order him back down to earth. These camera movements, with which Mankiewicz wanted to prove he was a fully-fledged director, don't so much construct a filmic space before the viewers' eyes as communicate enthusiastically, and link the various elements of the film. They display the shadowy presence of the director, as a gaze.

And we have a confession: 'I was a neurotic gambler, and what I didn't throw away I spent on boats. I dislike water, I almost never swim, I can't bear the cold water; but I was never happier than when I was on one of my boats sailing out over the ocean, heading away from shore. The only other time I felt that way was on the set. There I was boxed in, protected, away from it all in the land of make-believe where nothing really existed.'

It's what the retired ghost of Captain Gregg calls 'second-hand seafaring', when he looks at the sea through his telescope. As an answer to Lucy Muir's question as to what drives men to go to sea, away from the houses they have just built, why the ship's planks mean the world to him, he dictates the book to her – she dreams up his reply.

HACKS AND WHORES: SCREENWRITING

The film was only a moderate success when it was released in America. Mankiewicz explained this by saying that his apprentice-piece, rather than having the stylistic coherence that might have been achieved by an *auteur*, possessed only the uniformity of a studio production moulded by Zanuck. Philip Dunne blames the screenplay: 'The basic trouble in the script is that once the ghost drops out of the story, it tends to sag, and we had to go through a series of big lapses to get him in again at the end. That was the weakness inherent in the book, and there was really no way to solve it.'

The novel itself doesn't have these problems, because the ghost, for good reasons which are different from the film version, only disappears from the story momentarily, never definitively, and the idea of collaborating on a book only appears in the second part of the novel, after Lucy's unhappy affair with the ladies' man Miles Fairley. The problems the screenplay encountered arose first from the adaptation of the novel for the cinema, which made a visual spectacle out of an

internalised, aural story, secondly from the fact that a women's novel, a female fantasy of self-discovery with a good few drily comic overtones, had to be transformed into a passionate love story, in line with the 40s Hollywood idea of what constituted a successful women's film. Rather than being seen, twofold, as a squatter, the character of the woman becomes a male fiction, a mere reiteration of the old formula expressed by the irritable publisher Sproule: 'Twenty million discontented females in the British Isles, unhappily, are writing novels.'

Rex Harrison, at the time not quite forty and under contract to Fox, is the perfect match for the attractive young widow. He plays a retired captain who, in the book, is too old for the sea, 'short in sight and wind, slower in thought and movement'.

The author of the novel, Leslie, and her book meet the same fate as Mrs Muir when she tries to place the book with a publisher. Women write women's fiction, cookery books or, at best, fictional biographies of romantic poets.

Not that a more respectful treatment of the little novel would have yielded a better film. It was, indeed, the book's good fortune that no one involved really felt responsible as an author. This meant that the material could go on working autonomously, with resistances, gaps and inconsistencies. The rushes of the first few days' shooting suggest that Mankiewicz was closer to the author's intentions than Dunne. 'Haunted, how perfectly fascinating,' says Lucy with delight, completely reversing the standard scenarios involving haunted houses, where masochistic women are usually victims. Mrs Muir loves the house at first sight, 'as if the house itself would welcome me, asking me to rescue it from being so empty'.

But then Mankiewicz did after all behave like a director working to contract and Dunne as Zanuck's hack writer: 'To put it bluntly, a screenwriter is basically a hack. It cannot be otherwise, as long as motion pictures remain a *collaborative* art. A screenwriter at best is a stylistic chameleon, he writes in the style of the original source.'

The film is detached, like a pastiche, and Dunne's treatment comes as close to English women's literature as he was able to get. In the first third of the novel Lucy and the captain have an intimate conversation that shows them at their most harmonious. '"Oh, Lucia," the captain said softly, "you are so little and so lovely, how I should have liked to have taken you to Norway and shown you the fiords in

the midnight sun, and to China – what you have missed, Lucia, by being born too late to travel the Seven Seas with me! And what I've missed too." ' In the film, poetically embellished, these are the captain's words of farewell to the sleeping Lucy. He speaks them emphatically, as if reciting a poem, in order to legitimise the improbable invention of the entire film as a dream.

Just as Dunne relies on English women's fiction, Mankiewicz draws on the repertoire of the ghost film genre for scenes like the one in which Lucy, on her first meeting with the ghost, descends, a candle in her hand, into the crypt – the kitchen. Disinterestedly as Mankiewicz directs this scene, it reveals that genre conventions are the fundamental abstract formulae of the cinema.

By his own account, Mankiewicz also learned his approach to the cinema and his trade from the hacks, in the days of silent film, around the time of the changeover to sound, when the writing of a film was divided between two people, one of them responsible for continuity, the other for dialogue – men who were incapable of writing a decent letter, but who were 'nevertheless real writers in their own medium'. Mankiewicz was convinced that a new kind of writing had emerged with and for the cinema, one which altered the artistic function of language and its relationship to the audience as practised by the novel and the theatre. It assimilated certain visual and staging devices, and addressed the audience directly as a spoken language in actual voices which called for a response. Which is why Mankiewicz, even in the films that he only produced, exerted more influence on dialogue than on plot.

When I was finishing my studies, a writer was somebody who conceived and created the whole of a novel, a poem or a play, but who couldn't call himself a writer until he had sold his work: the novel, the poem or the play didn't exist until they were published, or acted. With the arrival of the sound film a completely new job emerged. A writer was engaged to write, or to adapt the work of others, and he was paid by the week. And he could rely on his income, even if the completed work wasn't what the client wanted.

The forms of marketable writing in Hollywood were shaped not only by production methods, but at least as much by those who delivered them, by the imported East Coast writers who despised their work for film, who hid their shame behind cynicism, although what they had done before in newspaper offices in New York and Chicago had also been unoriginal hack work.

Mankiewicz, not so much out of conformism as out of an insight into the specific nature of his work, didn't see its reproductive nature as discreditable, but more as something required by the medium: 'I'm not good at "originals". I have to start off with something, some plot situation; then I rework it in my own language and my own form.'

Despite his being obliged to respect Dunne's screenplay, Mankiewicz's interventions, his reworkings and rewrites, quite apart from those specifically mentioned by Dunne, are often apparent at many points as a third or fourth reading of the subtext. It would never have occurred to the captain as conceived by Leslie to quote poetry, certainly not Keats' *Ode to a Nightingale*. This is one of a series of references to English romanticism with which the film tries to evoke the aura of the female imagination, maybe even the memory, in educated viewers, of lines like 'the viewless wings of Poesy ... I have been half in love with easeful Death ... Was it a vision or a waking dream?'

Mankiewicz certainly chose this poem because it contains the line which became the title of Fitzgerald's novel *Tender is the Night*. Mankiewicz had rewritten Fitzgerald's dialogue for *Three Comrades* to make it more filmic, and had provoked enraged protests from him. 'If I go down at all in literary history, in a footnote, it will be as the swine who rewrote F. Scott Fitzgerald.'

Adapting Miss Leslie's novel for the cinema involved more than the usual problems of visualisation; because Mrs Muir in the book doesn't see ghosts, she hears the captain's voice inside her. 'The voice was not really there, she did not hear it with her ears. It seemed to come straight into her mind like thought.'

The intentions of the adapters, who were aiming at a predominantly female audience, required a radical restructuring, whose details speak for themselves. The location is no longer a lonely, forbidding stone house, but a sunny Californian building made of lightweight materials. In the novel the captain doesn't demand that Lucy put his portrait in her bedroom; she does it of her own accord and

Lucy, about to undress, covers the captain's portrait

thus in her imagination she breaks the great taboo. In the Hollywood love story, when the same thing happens at his command, it is the kind of suggestive circumvention of the censor of which Lubitsch was such a master.

In the book, in order to clarify to herself how she is to make sense of the captain's voice – and so that Leslie can do the same thing for her readers – Mrs Muir goes to an analyst, who proposes that she sublimate and rationalise the voice. But Mrs Muir has her own ideas about how she can put to rest the unruly ghost within herself. That will be the book.

In order to externalise this inward-looking female perspective, which is not hysterical, immediate identification, the classic Hollywood film needs a concert of differentiated voices. It needs a story with realised characters, because it cannot imagine any other way of attracting and holding an audience. This means that the film strays close to the boundaries of plausibility, and the audience's credulity nearly becomes active reflection about the medium and narration, in order for the film to work.

Fairley has stolen a handkerchief from Mrs Muir so that he can arrange to see her again.

FAIRLEY: Life is just one coincidence after another.
LUCY: Thank you for returning my handkerchief.
FAIRLEY: I feel ashamed of having taken it.
LUCY: You should be.
FAIRLEY: Only as a writer, of course. It is much too obvious a device.
LUCY: And in questionable taste.

The film allows itself very deliberate allusions both to the cinema as materialised shadow-play, and to its ephemeral images which fade like dreams. It indulges in pedantic explanations and doublings that are close to caricature. Next to the portrait of the captain 'which doesn't do him justice' there hangs a second painting, by Miles Fairley, of Mrs Muir in a bathing costume. And as if one book, *Blood and Swash*, through which a woman acquires masculine independence, were not

The painting of Lucy in the bathing costume

enough, Miles Fairley, the sarcastic swindler, has to write children's books. Lucy's little daughter Anna also has her own affair with an old sea-dog and fatherly friend, who carves her name into a kind of wooden gravestone, so deeply that neither sea nor time can affect it, and it will remain 'forever and a day'.

The ghost discreetly withdraws from Lucy's life because he no longer wants to stand in the way of her relationships with the living, after he has displayed thoroughly earthly jealousy towards his rival. In the book he is only there when she allows him to be. He is the fatherly friend, and 'there is nothing lover-like about him'. The analyst contradicts this with the Freudian view of negation. He sees Mrs Muir's assertion as the conscious repression of her natural instincts.

THE HAUNTED HOUSE UPSIDE DOWN
....

All the props for a gothic film are in place, made available by the genre and conjuring up a kind of *déjà vu*: the lonely house by the sea, full of secrets, almost in mid-air, in an intermediate realm; the interloper, a woman alone, a young widow shrouded in fluttering black veils; instead of the imposing ancestral portraits, the painting of the previous owner, a captain who is supposed to have committed suicide. Even the ending of the film fits in with the conventional framework of the genre: finally united, the couple leave the scene of the action on which the plot has been played out, although, in an inversion of the marriage formula, it is death that unites them.

Despite her youthful appearance, Mrs Muir is not a young creature tossed back and forth by sexual fears and desires as in Daphne du Maurier's *Rebecca*. She is not a victim of her imagination and hallucinations, she enjoys them. She has been through a marriage and has a little daughter – in the book a revolting son as well, who, with his sexist prejudices, is the embodiment of the conformist male world. Mrs Muir dreams a lot, and enjoys it, but she dreams with pleasure and without a bad conscience. Very early in the film, clock time is pointedly switched to film time; an hour flies past, the clock strikes four, and a second later it is five. Two clock faces merge.

Mrs Muir's projections, inspired by the house, return to the past and at the same time form the basis for her new life. Her backward-looking tendencies do not stop the film from advancing in a movement which, underlined by Bernard Herrmann's music, is like an ebb and flow.

Despite widow's weeds and the deaths before the story begins, there is nothing morbid about the atmosphere of the film, and after her first meeting with the ghost of Captain Gregg, Mrs Muir is resolved not to find her new life a sad one. The topoi and iconography of gothic films are there, but they function in an inverted way. Mrs Muir isn't as innocent as she pretends to be.

The idea of giving a burlesque reading of the story was beyond Gene Tierney's acting capabilities, and Mankiewicz did not yet have the experience and independence – as he later did in *Sleuth* – to play fast and loose with a genre.

The old house, which in the gothic genre always becomes the spatialisation of the identity problem, becomes her refuge from the prison of conventions. She has the feeling it wants to be rescued by her. Its ghost becomes her confidant and her accomplice in freeing herself from any remaining fetters of marriage.

She doesn't freeze under the captain's gaze like the heroine of Hitchcock's *Suspicion* under the eye of her military father. Her fantasies set the frozen painting in motion. She dismantles it. 'The painting doesn't do you justice,' she tells the ghost, and to her cook Martha she voices doubts about his suicide. Finally, she dissolves the painted portrait into the story she writes about him. Thus she brings the revenant to rest. She rehabilitates the bad reputation of the house by dreaming up a rather unworthy father figure.

The painted portraits that appear so often in the American films of the 40s do not reflect the status of the cinematic image in comparison with painting. They relate to the altered function of the referent in the sign-system of the cinema. Documented reality becomes fictional. For *Laura*, Preminger did not refuse Gene Tierney's painted portrait because it was simply too bad for him as a connoisseur and collector of art, but because it was no use in his film. The painterly photograph that he did use is not a portrait of Laura, but refers to Tierney as the model.

....

Freud's famous question about the crucial difference, about what women want, is countered in *The Ghost and Mrs Muir* with another question, with the desire to know what drives men to take to the sea. The ideal father, the standard for the men who come after him, is quite figuratively brought from his symbolic position down into realistic dimensions, and, among other things, provided with qualities by the loving daughter which are normally considered to be stereotypical characteristics of femininity.

The captain is permanently impassioned and lacking in self-control, as is expressed in his manner of communication, which tends to consist of curses and turns his exhibited authority into a rant. He can't write, and when speaking he needs help with his grammar. He claims the right to be more natural, following his instincts, and therefore to have lived a more fulfilled life. She, on the other hand, uses language in a more detached manner, precisely because she doesn't have a language of her own. She appropriates male language, and uses its effects to her advantage.

The captain is not only given female characteristics. It's childish of him, Mrs Muir tells him, to play jokes on the people who visit the house as if he were a goblin. She alters the great custom: the father is brought up by the daughter.

The boundary between ghostly phenomena and realistic images, on which Zanuck insisted for commercial reasons, turns the captain into a kind of Nosferatu, for whom walls, doors and windows are no obstacle. But above all it realises the invincible obstacle that stands between Mrs Muir and the object of her desire. 'Keep your distance, madam,' the ghost brusquely repels her when, in a rush of intimacy, she comes too close to him. That is like the line used by Lubitsch at the end of *Design for Living*; it has the same effect on the viewer as the famous 'No Sex'.

....

Gothic stories written by women in the nineteenth century, whose limited range of characters and unchanging locations suggest archaic family constellations, were the feminine equivalent of the *Bildungsroman*, introspective and written as if by a sleepwalker.

If we consider the sparse historical indices in *The Ghost and Mrs Muir*, the film and the novel, it is noticeable and symptomatic that they both fail to mention the First World War. This in itself marks out the time of the film as asocial, internal time. What the *noir* women's films of the 40s register of the crises in gender relationships sparked by the war is, in *Mrs Muir*, determined rather by the English gothic genre and transposed into an ahistorical past, into that time which corresponds to psychic investigation. Mrs Muir in the novel, to be sure that her ghostly communication has nothing to do with a possible mid-life crisis, even finds herself an analyst. The film could not make use of that, because the effect would have been too realistic and too contemporary.

Mankiewicz himself underwent analysis with Otto Fenichel, a member of Freud's innermost Viennese circle, which he still recalled as a torment when, as an old man, he spoke in front of Michel Ciment's camera. Mankiewicz was well known for wildly analysing his actresses and wives, or putting them in touch with analysts. The possibility of representing the fused time of analysis became the actual subject of his films and, closely connected with that, the relation between the sexes. Their particular orientation towards the past identifies their time as the time of anamnesis. They are not backward-looking, but they do seek an anchorage in the past. Just as past and present cannot be separated in his films, the behaviour of his characters is not unambiguously gender-specific, although he purports to be on the track of women's femininity.

Mrs Muir's ghost is a visualised form of flashback, the trademark of all later Mankiewicz films. It is an early sign that his flashbacks are not merely a narrative device, but a continuing engagement with time in the cinema, in which for him image and language tend to pull in different directions.

> I don't believe in the flashback as a sort of 'trick'. It should only be used when it is impossible to tell a story in the present without referring to the past. I hope that one day it will be possible to tell the present and the past together, at the same time. ... We're so preoccupied with trying out new surface effects that we haven't yet started to use those devices that are profoundly those of the screen. (Mankiewicz, in *Cahiers du Cinéma*, May 1966.)

The ghost of Captain Gregg is a form of filmic presence condensing itself. The first time he appears he is just a silhouette, the shadow of a broad back, pushing its way into the picture and obscuring the audience's view of the sleeping Mrs Muir. The second time, in the dark kitchen at night, it looks as though Mrs Muir is forcing him to reveal himself with a 'fiat' gesture of her candle. The shadow cast by his appearance is as sharp as a paper cut-out and strikingly unrealistic in the way it falls.

The film itself, in sound and image, provides the viewer with keywords for the treatment of the phenomena on the screen. Mrs Muir is in intimate conversation with the captain in broad daylight when the 'blasted inlaws' turn up. Mrs Muir urges the ghost to hide, disappear, decompose. The captain corrects her: dematerialise. And it is more to remind the viewer how precarious and artificial is the life of the shadowy creatures on the screen when he tells Mrs Muir, by way of explanation, 'They can't see me or hear me unless I choose that they should.'

When a ghost dematerialises in the cinema it demonstrates all the more what material it is made of. The images on the screen are interspersed with orchestrated gazes, which are detached from the characters, and which lead out of the film. Rather than reflecting reality, they look. Rather than simply recording the visual, they subvert it.

Since film started talking, its ghosts are no longer what they once were in the silent cinema. They have changed along with developments in film technology. Captain Gregg is something in between the ghost that was originally supposed to pursue Spencer Tracy in *Fury* – Mankiewicz, as Lang's producer, cut him out – and the voice of Addie Ross in Mankiewicz's own *Letter to Three Wives*, which forces its way in between her acquaintances as a perverse kind of voice-over, semi-incarnate, both screen interference and flea in the ear.

The cinema uses ghosts to embody what is missing from the pictures. It turns this lack to its own advantage, and turns it into an engine of its invention. It isn't just that a mute inner life is given visible form. What it cannot – or may not – represent appears in images of quite particular visual intensity. The entire reality is only what the eye makes of it.

THE MOST FORWARD GENTLEMAN
· ·

'You are the most obstinate woman I ever met,' one of the two men says to her, and the other says, 'Oh, Lucia, you are so little and so lovely.' In between there lies an entire programme of ideas of femininity, a solid foundation for a film story aimed chiefly at a female audience. We also know that gothic stories by women authors, whether determined by fear or desire, are love stories, women's favourite fictional genre, corresponding to their own range of experience and their fantasies of self-assertion. But Lucy doesn't want a man. She wants to be a man, to be able to speak effectively like a man, to be free like a man.

George Sanders, the old tom-cat, as Miles Fairley, immediately sets off in pursuit of the object of his desire. Mrs Muir turns out to be an author, and as if to protect himself he assumes she is a writer of cook books, or possibly of a life of Byron – which is not a reference to the early days of women's emancipation in the story-telling movement, but a way of exploiting the cliché of romantic women for the general mood of the film – or of a book about dreams. Thus is the idea of women's literature summed up. In comparison, a male author, however limited he may be, has the advantage that his gender speaks for him when he writes. Mrs Muir gets her revenge, with an incredulous smile, when he is forced to admit that, however ill it sits with his outward appearance and his behaviour, he makes his living from children's books.

Miles Fairley: 'Surprising enough to find a lady author infinitely more exciting than her heroines could possibly be.' Once again, in a movement typical of the film, the visible is extended by the gaze that falls upon it.

The weary publisher Sproule, who would himself rather have gone to sea than prostitute himself in the service of family and business, in pursuit of money, tries to send Mrs Muir packing by observing that 'twenty million discontented females' in the British Isles think they have to write a novel.

Because it is not properly speaking written, Mrs Muir's book is not literature but recorded speech, a sailor's yarn, autobiography, whose beginning, middle and end has been written by life itself. The novelist writes of it: 'Lucy could hear his voice moving up and down the room, as if he were walking a quarter-deck. She tried to picture him as a young man ...' The film provides its own explanation, an orthodox Freudian one, of typical female intellectual activity, of daydreams, the product of inactivity and isolation. 'I dreamt my book, I never could have thought of it,' Mrs Muir tells her by now grown-up daughter.

Sproule's and Fairley's ideas are themselves embellished interpretations of the novel, wild imaginings invented specially for the film by a team believing that they are satisfying the expectations and desires of women. Supposedly mediating, they interpose their projections between author and female viewers, an attempt to turn the clock back – as happened everywhere after the Second World War when women who had become more independent were returned to their pre-war social status, the private sphere.

Crucial lines in the novel are transferred to other characters, so that they fit more easily with the love story idea, and certain images and qualities are also taken over but assigned to different people. The amazon mentioned in the novel is not Lucy, rechristened Lucia by the captain, but the cook who, armed with broom and bucket, puts the scruffy house in order.

But even more far-reaching is the rewriting strategy employed in the film, in which lines are added in for members of the opposite sex in order to restore the sexual balance, the mirror-image of the genders with which the classic Hollywood film operates. The novel does not end with the couple finally united in death, striding rejuvenated into an eternal future, but with the corpse of a woman who has died lonely but not unhappy, shedding her physical shell as a snake sloughs its old skin, insinuating a cyclical view of time rather than a linear, goal-oriented story. 'The body of the little Mrs Muir sat very still in the chair, the face tilted sideways, looking without seeing into the painted eyes of Captain Gregg's portrait on the wall.' A painting, however successful it may be from the artistic point of view, is excessive perception which, as a positive form of illusion, overcomes in imagination what separates people.

The boundary seemingly made more subtle just for the censor, which, covered by the essential difference between the partners, permits their illegitimate cohabitation under one roof and even in the bedroom, opens up other possible interpretations, particularly because of its ambivalence. It contains even richer connotations, for the pleasure of the female audience in particular. It produces an all-pervasive sensuality that does not constantly seek a substitute for the real thing in the fleeting image. We should not forget that in both film and novel the happy association between man and woman derives from the book they have written together. In a material sense it is a love story. Thought up by a woman with a man in the role of the muse. Eroticism extended by words and by representation.

He thinks it is old-maidish prudery when she balks at typing a notorious four-letter word. She visibly stumbles over the word, which is given physical presence by dint of its indirectness. She breaks it down into individual letters. What remains of the body of the word, as if distilled, is its sound.

In a popular genre and a popular medium, with a director who is not yet a strong *auteur*, more demands are made on the viewer than in an aesthetically assured work in search of uniqueness. The film's constant references to light, images, eyes and vision can be seen as self-reflection of the medium. But they are probably intended to remind the viewer of the pact made at the start, to take daydreams as seriously as reality. The story is not concerned with the familiar. The film requires the viewer to make the effort of extending the concept of reality into the invisible.

Mrs Muir embodies the unprofessional imagination of the viewer. What she invents is as original and popular as dreams. She also gives concrete form to an idea of writing as an activity of simulation which only becomes possible through a degree of distance. By way of this dissociation, Mrs Muir becomes the author of her own life. That is not only a paradox, it is heartbreaking.

In the novel the ghostly captain explains what it means to have a vivid imagination: it is an unoriginal ability to be receptive to alien points of view, and be ready to think with them.

Mrs Muir wonders why she can see him when he has no physical shell. His answer as explanation to Mrs Muir also refers the viewer, who was about to abandon all rationality and yield utterly to the fiction, back to his or her place outside the fiction: 'All you see is an illusion, a blasted lantern slide.' Zanuck thought the audience adult enough to accept the break in illusion. That is, the camera, the director, everyone acts as though their senses too were deceiving them. The viewer is invited to identify not so much with the characters on the screen as with the gaze that falls upon them.

Zanuck's decision is a direct consequence of the previous one with regard to the screenplay, to undertake a cinematic shift of register, a change of senses – because Mrs Muir in the novel never sees the captain, she hears him as an inner voice: 'But that night the captain refused to be put off. "I must speak to you, Lucia," he said, and his voice thundered through her senses, shaking her to answer him. "Well," she said, admitting him to her consciousness since he would not be denied.'

But in the cinema, how does one create, against all pictorial objectivity, a subjective, imaginary, internal image that allows two heterogeneous systems of perception to co-exist? The violence inherent in Zanuck's solution means that the perspective of the film is a usurped one. The images that we see are the monstrous offspring of a female imagination in opposition to all the rules of cinema. Camera and director try to follow as best they can, by adopting her point of view. The camera has to achieve this through its mobility, as it does with the first appearance of the ghost, when Lucy only dreams his presence. The director repeats what Mrs Muir does when she speaks with a man's voice in her book, with a form of differentiated doubling.

There is, invented by God knows who, a category of women's directors. They don't limit themselves to bringing a greater understanding to their treatment of women's themes. In their films, objectifying visuality is dissolved by movement. It is a liberation from the gender-defined cinema of identification. This was already present in the silent film, in the work of Murnau, who implicated the camera in the events on screen, and with Dreyer's 'gliding close-ups'. But with the arrival of sound in Renoir and Mizoguchi, Ophüls and Antonioni, an element of movement in another register was added.

How, Dreyer wondered during the shooting of *Vampyr*, does one manage to give images the additional dimension of the gaze without arresting their natural course? How, in a visual medium, can the *way* a person sees be added to what is seen?

> Imagine that we are sitting in an ordinary room. Suddenly we are told that there is a corpse behind the door. In an instant, the room we are sitting in is completely altered; everything in it has taken on another look; the light, the atmosphere have changed, though they are physically the same.

Even if the script attempts to reduce what the novel portrayed as imagination to a simple love story, the decision to treat the imaginary as something entirely normal salvages some of the author's intentions. In front of the images there remains the possibility of a different gaze.

IMAGES SET TO MUSIC AND TO WORDS

At first glance, particularly with its reading of the novel through visualisation at any price, the film demonstrates the omnipotence of cinematic images. Only gradually does it become apparent that they are threatened by a latent asynchrony, by sounds that don't match them. Sounds that are in the air or just air, nothing but atmosphere, by presences without bodies – little Anna's dog, its ears cocked, becomes aware of them first. With the help of insistent sounds they condense into illusions which are ultimately nothing but embodied inner voices, repressed thoughts, doctored feelings.

The ghost first manifests itself in ringing laughter, when Mrs Muir utters a half-formed thought in which the word 'clean' occurs. The clock that announces his first, still shadowy appearance on screen is framed like a ship's wheel. It doesn't ring out the hours like a normal clock, but with the double beat of a ship's bell – it measures out Lucy's dream-time with a dissolve.

From the opening credits onwards, the ear is claimed by Bernard Herrmann's surging music, which was, unusually, allowed to replace the Fox signature tune. It heralds something that will become quite unambiguous in later sequences: in a reversal of the usual relationship between image and sound, stressing the gulf between what is heard and what is seen, the music at times gets the upper hand and often determines the point of view of the scene more firmly than the camera's organisation of the scene. It assumes the role of narration, like a voice off, and suggests the idea of separate worlds, of separate spaces.

Years later, talking about his music for Brian De Palma's *Obsession*, Herrmann recalled: 'I identified with the girl, how she felt … The only other score I ever felt this way about was *The Ghost and Mrs Muir*; there's the same feeling of aloneness, of solitude.'

In the latter part of the film, when the passing years and

spreading loneliness outgrow the images, it is the music rather than the action that determines their course. In a sequence of shots of the sea lashed by autumn storms, the music practically takes off from the images – like the scene in which the prosaic film dialogue passes over into the poetic momentum of Keats' *Ode to a Nightingale*, and once again, when the captain bids farewell to the sleeping Lucy and Rex Harrison, assuming an imposing monologue stance, explicitly turns to address his words of farewell to the camera. He becomes nothing but voice as his image slowly dissolves in the only ghostly superimposition in the film. 'The dream will die as all dreams must die at wakening.' His words also threaten the film's images.

Herrmann later used this sea music in his opera *Wuthering Heights*, for the storm scene which concludes the second act. It is wild music, characteristic of Herrmann's relationship towards English romanticism and romantic women's literature. It celebrates the unruly power of the imagination – not a pale idea of nature in harmony with the passive world of female emotion. 'I have no real direction in life, I am seeking for the intangibles, I look for poetry and dreams of life, not for the realities.' Three years before *The Ghost and Mrs Muir*, Herrmann had written the music for Robert Stevenson's film version of *Jane Eyre*.

Studies of the language of the English women's novel have shown that women without a language of their own turned to dialect and professional jargon to avoid male literary language, and also to avoid writing the way women were expected to write.

Herrmann describes film music as 'a strange kind of masquerading form of art' matching his own re-echoing talent which never developed into a distinctive voice. Like Mankiewicz, the rewriter, he was aware of the unoriginality of his film work. His score for Mankiewicz's film is equally empathetic and playful in its use of quotations. It runs parallel with the movement of the film as a whole. The most effective way of circumventing conventions is to show that it is possible to imitate supposedly natural arrangements, to reveal them for the artifice they really are. Even tragic feelings are rather cheaper in the cinema than in the old, original arts. Which is not to say that something that is not unique is by definition soulless.

In an interview in *Sight and Sound*, Herrmann explained that from his years of working for the radio he had learned to achieve dramatic effects without reference to images. Perhaps Mrs Muir's ghost is also a wireless invention inspired by the radio, a voice from another world interfering with the images. Radio, at any rate, introduced new ideas of possibly different relations between image and sound.

Herrmann's music carries all those things of the imagination that cannot be imagined, everything that really resists visual depiction. It embodies liberating movement in emphatic opposition to the painted pictures in front of which, staring and stared at, the characters again and again stand and conduct conversations.

In women's films with love stories the excessive use of music is a narrative convention and a clichéd expression of emotional, irrational female behaviour. In *The Ghost and Mrs Muir* it carries not only the emotions but also at times the story itself. The spirit world, the inner world, despite the changes made to the novel, remains linked to sounds. Through the music, which imitates the tides as a repetitive leitmotif, the time of the narrative is also deflected from its linear, teleological course. Since the leitmotifs do not refer to particular people and places, they help to erase the boundaries between objective and subjective world. The music generalises time into a feeling of time, merging the different temporal layers. 'Forever and a day,' old seaman Scroggins tells his

'Forever and a day,' old seaman Scroggins tells Anna

little friend Anna, her name will still be legible carved deep in that piece of wood.

Herrmann's music also realises the old metaphor of the spinning weave of time. At the end of the film it is as if a web has been spun around Mrs Muir. Slowly the contours of Gene Tierney's familiar features disappear behind white make-up, until the mummified becomes the beautiful young girl once more.

We don't know who first suggested Herrmann as composer for the film. Given Mankiewicz's ambition to match the achievements of his big brother Herman, he was probably not uninvolved in the choice. The first film music that Herrmann wrote was for *Citizen Kane*, scripted by Herman Mankiewicz, who won an Oscar for it.

Herrmann and Mankiewicz shared an enthusiasm for all things English. With a carefully selected cast, including Rex Harrison, Edna Best, George Sanders, Robert Coote and Whitford Kane, the film is a concert of English tones. Gene Tierney's often vain attempts at English pronunciation do nothing to hamper the film's intentions. The English tones of the film have by no means a naturalistic function. The important thing with Tierney was the oscillation between an affected, proper tone and her lapses into seaman's talk. Her English only needs to be a register, a cliché of Englishness. She in any case plays a woman who is imbued with the desire to lead her own life, but who does not have a language of her own.

Mankiewicz prided himself on inventing W. C. Fields' famous routine of ornithological forms of address, the 'little tomtits' and 'magpies' and 'chickadees'. According to Michael Caine, who acted in his last film, he knew how to make words visible. Sometimes he even plays jokes with them, adding in the image afterwards, as if in evidence of the word. The ghost boasts to Mrs Muir that he has solved all her financial problems, all she will have to do is write a book. A book! She is horrified, and promptly an entire bookcase appears behind her – the viewer is naturally free to conclude that Mrs Muir has made this suggestion herself.

By making words visible, Mankiewicz turns them into a source of aesthetic pleasure because he shows them as a means of seduction. For this reason his scripts need experienced actors who know how to juggle with words, regardless of their appearance, like Rex Harrison, whom he called his Stradivarius.

'The word you are looking for is "brass"', Miles Fairley tells the horrified and delighted Mrs Muir. Miles/Sanders is not a matinee idol, not a great looker, he is a *beau parleur*, what Lubitsch would call 'a schmuser'. He does it with words, which captivate Lucy: 'You must be a magician.' She is partly referring to his false, artificial notes, to the charm of which she gladly succumbs. The battle for Lucy's favours is fought out by two voices, two different ways of talking. It is not true, as the captain maintains, making claims for his own unimpeachable honesty, that Lucy – like all women – was blindly taken in.

All Mankiewicz's films contain a character who acts as his spokesman, his mouthpiece. Admittedly he said that of the films he had written himself. But we should simply allow ourselves to see him through and behind Sanders. Philip Dunne has also confirmed that Mankiewicz rewrote these scenes.

A humorous interlude in the film, which does not exist in the novel in this form, is the visit of the tiresome relatives to Gull Cottage. In front of the women who are supposedly talking, acting and reacting normally, Lucy holds conversations with herself. She talks nonsense, and has adopted an unrespectable colloquial mode of speech. Their psychological explanations are no closer to the true situation than the visit is necessary for the development of the plot. The function of the scene is to show in images what is revealed through language, and to show how language encourages duplicity.

It also makes the viewer toe the line, on Lucy and the captain's side. It lures the viewer further into the fiction of the film and against common sense in the shape of the two ladies. 'What a hideous painting,' says the spinsterly sister-in-law, and even before the viewer has had time to compare the portrait and her profile – as everything in the shot encourages us to do – the visibly invisible captain intervenes and gives vent to Lucy's own immediate reaction.

This humorous moment for the audience's pleasure also plays with fire. In Zanuck's primarily realistic film, this spirit incarnate goes as far as Hollywood could allow in suggesting that film depends on an act of faith on the part of the audience.

In Mankiewicz's films people do not speak as they would on the stage, or in a novel, or in a careless, slangy manner. He does not write easily digestible dialogue for the actors, so that they can slip as casually as possible into the plot. The viewer is supposed to take note of them, listen, connect himself through what is said with what is shown. He would like to make films for thinking people about banal intellectual activity, about the theatre of everyday life.

> The horror of a coffin lid opening is masturbation; what interests me is the uncontrollable, the emotions that suddenly take possession of a man when he didn't know they were in him. What interests me is the screenplays that people write every day, the lies they constantly tell one another, the game they play at every moment, and how they end up prisoners of their own lies. And women have had to perfect a much greater variety of lies, deceptions, substitutes, ersatz egos, than men.

What he does to the images by way of language – 'I'm an iconoclast' – is in contradiction to his statements and in part to his filmic practices, with which he defends classic Hollywood dramaturgy, the transparent image from which, so as not to disturb the viewer's consumption of its story, all traces of the film's production have been expunged.

> If in the course of a film a trick, a shot, an angle, an editing effect makes a viewer nudge his neighbour and ask him, 'How did they do that?', or 'What a terrific shot!', the whole film is ruined. For me a film's *raison d'être* is to transport the audience either out of reality or into reality, whichever; that's what it has to do, it has to absorb all of the viewer's attention. If the film-maker interposes himself, he destroys the effect of reality.

He doesn't seem afraid of the endless reflection of the images, prompted by the opening of the closed pictorial space by the spoken word, as a break with illusion. He believes in the persuasiveness of language, which connects the outer and inner world, making a more complete picture of reality. Theatre was unable to do this, because it had only words and bodies at its disposal, and could only hint at the outside world in the distance, in the stage-set. In the cinema everything is within reach, on a single level. And just as his flashbacks do not lead back into the past, but show the past remaining effective in the present, language, supported by the movements of cinema, amplifies the events of the plot into something more than stories.

The Ghost and Mrs Muir is still too much story, and a narrative trick is required to realise imagination and the workings of the mind. But in the end Mrs Muir does not write the captain's life story under his dictation. Obstinate as she is, she has – and we must not forget this for a moment – imagined the lover herself.

MAN IN THE PICTURE IS WOMAN IN THE MIRROR

When the film was released in 1947 it didn't make much of an impression on the wider audience or, consequently, at the box office. The critics were condescending about Dunne's screenplay and Tierney's acting. The direction of a film of this kind was not an issue anyway.

Twenty-five years later, Mankiewicz's biographer Kenneth Geist suggested that Mankiewicz, by skilful modulation, gives the illusion that Tierney's inept beauty actually possessed range and technique. A writer in *Film Comment* recently suggested that chemical reactions between the film's emotional ingredients had turned the film into something more complex and fascinating than its producers – who wanted to make a weepie – could have hoped for.

In France things were different from the start, because in that country it wasn't the wider audience but cinephiles and intellectuals who shaped the reception of postwar American cinema and remodelled it. The film's *sujet* and *mise-en-scène* had been briefly but thoroughly dealt with in *Gazette du Cinéma*, the predecessor of *Cahiers du Cinéma*, at the time of the film's release. It was discussed more recently when retrospectives of Mankiewicz's films encouraged people to take another look at his early works. And something else unimaginable in America also happened, which was related to the European need to make up for lost time after the war. Bertrand Tavernier plausibly describes it as a parallel development to the *politique des auteurs*: a *politique des actrices* arose. This also made of the film something different from what the studio had planned.

The French cult of the actress is quite unlike the attitude of American fans. It follows on the heels of the eroticism of the Surrealists, with their *culte de femme*. It is a truism that fetishisation occurs at the expense of women.

Les Aventures de Madame Muir became a film which sublimated Tierney's looks and movements: she is not a great actress, her impetus as an actress quickly falters, her diction is monotonous, but she is the personification of the photogenic. 'She was always adorable, often excellent, and in some films simply a genius.'

Whenever *Les Aventures de Madame Muir* is shown on French television, it isn't emotional women who get tears in their eyes, but eminent film theorists and film historians. If I didn't mention this inversion it would amount to suppressing a crucial piece of evidence. The phenomenon combines an image of what cinema once was and the glamour of a woman. And both are promised eternal youth and beauty by the film's ending. (I beg forgiveness for the indiscretion of publishing private confessions.)

'What inelegance,' one of Tierney's most fervent admirers said of a woman writer who apostrophised her as a star *a posteriori* and tried to understand her magic by analysing its individual parts. The writer concluded that Tierney's seemingly contradictory features, an opaque mask-like quality, fertile ground for every kind of fantasy, in conjunction with a helpless sensuality, determined the roles in which she was cast and the consequent construction of her image – plus some appropriate dramatic details from her private life.

In her autobiography, *Self Portrait*, Tierney describes herself as a frontier girl, constantly switching sides and camps as if sleepwalking; divided and inconsistent, caught between two worlds. And rather than seeking the roots of her private misfortunes in the star system, in the visual marketing of herself – completely misjudging the nature of her professional abilities – she writes: 'I had no trouble playing any kind of role. My problem began when I had to be myself.' She could have learned from R. A. Dick's Mrs Muir that the understanding of one's own divided nature is no bad guide in life, and masquerades – Mrs Muir even uses her mourning clothes in this way – are not manoeuvres designed to deceive but a subversive deployment of signs which undermine the predominant symbolic codes. We need only consider the use of the clothes articulating the bodies to understand whose visual pleasure *The Ghost and Mrs Muir* is designed to satisfy.

Captain Gregg is no common-or-garden poltergeist. We see that the first time he appears, not in Mrs Muir's dreams but in her kitchen, conjured by her irritated insults – who ever heard of a cowardly ghost?

He casts a clean, sharp shadow on the wall, something that ghosts, as we know, don't do. It is Mrs Muir's gaze, Gene Tierney's spotlight eyes, intensified by the light of the candle she holds up, that photographs him. It is her projection.

But that granted almost too much autonomy to the female imagination. Transferred from the auditory to the visual, the story was forced by the medium to become a love story, even if the captain regrets that he has neither a body nor fleshly desires. His clothes, always the same, turn him into a symbolic figure, upright, demanding attention, self-important, in dark trousers, roll-neck sweater, dark jacket with high, broad shoulders, with only a martial-looking belt-buckle to catch the eye. It's curious that we never see him in the cap he wears in the portrait. This is probably due to the refusal of the fashion-conscious Rex Harrison to wear it, thinking that peaked caps didn't suit his face, unless of course the ghost, without the cap as a token of power, was supposed to appear demoted.

It is he who – unseen – sees everything, and beneath his gaze, for him she becomes somebody. Growing to meet his expectations, she

Rex Harrison: 'a symbolic figure, upright, demanding attention'

moults from Lucy into Lucia. She doesn't look at the mirror to see herself, but with downcast eyes, in order to see how he sees her. What she later sees in the mirror, and what the viewer naturally does not see, when she coquettishly rearranges her hair in the train, is Fairley's gaze upon her, the gaze of the man who existed only in her imagination.

Jean-Louis Schefer asks whether images are mirrors, not in *L'homme ordinaire du cinéma* but in *La lumière et la proie*. They are mirrors, he's sure of it. Only 'they don't reflect our faces, but the things that we lack: the sublime. That's why the obscene, which we don't lack, is always incomplete in painting.'

With the star, with Gene Tierney, a woman to be looked at, a whole narrative strand is unwound, dealing with clothes, wardrobes, outfits. Fashion – and it isn't just the industry that lives off its constant change – is the epitome of feminine instability, which is momentarily consolidated by external approval of its outward appearance. Like everything in the film, clothing too is exhaustively discussed. That is, it is made visible through language in a detached way, and raised to the level of consciousness. The identificatory spell of images is broken. Of course clothes can reflect.

The wardrobe designed by Oleg Cassini for his wife, Gene Tierney, is all respectably Victorian, with little lace collars, crocheted shawls, ruching, plissées, fringes, braid and an awful lot of buttons. Only when Miles Fairley enters her life and she steps into nature does Lucy wear a white dress that flows and falls. The only extravagance that Cassini allowed himself is the feathered hat, the seagull hat, the nightingale hat, that Mrs Muir wears when she travels to London to place her book with a publisher. If the viewer has not yet taken sufficient notice of it, he cannot avoid doing so when Fairley remarks, 'Your hat is singularly inadequate under the circumstances.' The hat objectivises Tierney's facial traits by making her high cheekbones look even more exotic, and her usually credulous or diffusely beaming eyes look even intelligent and ironic.

Lucy in a bathing costume is an invention of the film, and its dramatic necessity is not at first evident. Fairley has already undressed her with his eyes far beyond what the bathing suit reveals. Martha thinks it scandalous that Fairley's painting should be on display to other people. Lucy talks about fetishes and taboos that ought to be jettisoned in the twentieth century. The expression doesn't sit easily with her

Gene Tierney's wardrobe: the little lace collars . . . ruching . . . fringes; a white dress that flows and falls; the feathered hat

character, even if it is supposed to contain an element of self-deception, and Tierney has difficulties in putting it across convincingly.

The bathing costume should be seen as an argument in the sequence of events which make up Lucy's attempts to liberate herself, the most effective one being her bid to play an intellectual 'breeches part', which enables her to escape things other than conventions. She puts gender-specific introspection and biologically based ideas of masculinity and femininity in doubt. She plays with these illusions with an expression of the purest innocence, and not only in the quiet of her room. She amuses herself with the written word. Supported by a dubious father-figure, she is playing with the law.

Her escape from the Victorian world fails. We can see why when the two women marked by marriage, the philanderer's two women, sit side by side rather than face to face on the sofa, corseted and buttoned in clothes which refuse to allow any freedom of movement, any play, but which demand posture from the wearer. Women were – and it is not easy to decide to what extent this really contradicted their own interests – supports and receptacles of Victorian morality.

The last part of the film, Mrs Muir's lonely death, cannot simply be interpreted as a resigned return to the old order. Let us once again refer to the novel to clarify an aspect of the film, the way in which Lucy ends her affair with Fairley.

> ... Lucy, gazing back at him still with this strange feeling of detachment. He could go from one play to another, always the central figure, always bringing down the curtain when comedy threatened to turn to tragedy or domesticity, leaving the other players stranded, to think out their own endings to their ruined plot; but, thought Lucy, it was she who held the book of this play and she would end it in her own manner.

A period picture by Mankiewicz can be seen, like his flashbacks, as a film-specific articulation of time. Before cinema it had never been possible to show how conserving life-forms tend to be, how hostile to development, and what non-synchronicities look like.

The film's happy ending doesn't bring the story to a close.

5 2   Lucy, recalling the ghost

THE AMBITION TO BE A PRODUCER/WRITER/DIRECTOR
....

It is said that Mankiewicz got the best performances out of his actresses if he had a relationship with them. The gossip has a deeper significance. It could enlighten us about the way in which, in the cinema, compared to individually based classical arts, the relation of author and work has changed in accordance with that of star and performance. The reality of bodies is implied in a different way. To the eye they are within reach, but they have never been more unattainable.

The Ghost and Mrs Muir is seen as romantic because it is supposedly a love story. It is romantic, because longing, male and female, pulling in opposite directions, is the unassuageable, empty centre of the story – the split is right in the middle of the story – and the power of fiction momentarily conquers this fundamental incompatibility. With romanticism, relations between the sexes became problematic. And women writers played their part in this, for they were beginning to articulate their otherness and shed an appropriate and brighter light on the cosy 'riddle of womanhood' of the male imagination, with which even Freud repressed the femininity that was problematic to him.

'With talk came the Jew' – this is Mankiewicz's description of the change that occurred in the film industry when talkies, and with them the need for speakable texts, led to the importation of members of the East Coast intelligentsia to the Hollywood studios. The fact that the bodies in silent films, so lifelike in other respects, were unable to speak, made them appear uncanny. The voices in the talkies never quite got over the fact that they were cut off from the bodies. They never really grew back together. Even when speech was synchronised it retained a belatedness and a degree of independence that resisted the subjection to the image that realism demanded.

For colloquial language this was a chance to become artificial. Influenced by technology, it was able to switch from a simply referential to a symbolic category. (Henry James speculated on the dissociation of body and language through the new media in his short story *In the Cage*.)

In contrast to the usual practices of the film industry, Mankiewicz deepens the rift between word and image, allowing language to predominate at the expense of the visual *mise-en-scène*: 'I am a film-heretic – anathema to those who find it so much easier to point a camera than direct an actor. I'm known to be committed to the heresy that the word can be at least as contributive to the non-epic films than the lens. I am also known to prefer actors trained in speaking to those who just grunt through hair. My films talk a lot – hell, I talk a lot.'

Eric Rohmer, in an enthusiastic essay on Mankiewicz's *The Quiet American* which he wrote years ago, was amazed at himself: Eric Rohmer, in *Cahiers*, unrestrainedly praising a film unconcerned with spatial construction and physical expression, whose director took not the slightest interest in *mise-en-scène* as advocated by *Cahiers*, nor in *écriture*! What he found so eminently filmic about this *cinéma impur*, this talk-cinema, is best revealed later by his own films. At the time he explained his approval in that this film fulfilled the necessary extension of the concept of *mise-en-scène*. That sound film directors should be expected to pay the same attention to staging language as they did to staging images. The cinema-specific integration of language was only complete when it functioned dynamically within the shot, when it became a necessary part and was not simply used to heighten the verisimilitude of the images. What the sound film needs, he writes, is a new *découpage*, a different continuity from that of the silent film, which still predominates in the talkies. Mankiewicz expressed this state of affairs by saying that 'the adaptation is the first part of the realisation.'

What Mankiewicz knows about speaking, and the way he uses talk as a means of action and not primarily as expression, he learned at least as much on the analyst's couch as at school and university. He films language as a physical driving force, thereby attacking the ideas and images of masculinity in the American cinema, which let the better half of the sound film go to waste: 'No, the man's role as presently in vogue doesn't interest me very much as writer and/or director. He is invariably expected to pit himself physically against his adversary: to me, the least imaginative form of confrontation.'

What can be done with words is not only manifested in the dialogue of his films. He already practised it on the set in his work with his actors, particularly the female ones, whom he persuaded through language to achieve things which didn't bring forth an illusory femininity but freed them from supposedly immutable bonds. He was interested in active women, scheming women, divided women: 'Performing women, I won't stop being fascinated and terrified by them; I won't stop thinking and learning and writing about them until I die.'

All About Eve is not about the eternal Eve and her fascinating and impenetrable secret. Eve is made up of as many women as there are female parts in the film. And another, surprising species. In one of his loquacious confessions, which every interview with him invariably turned into, Mankiewicz says that what drives Eve is not fundamentally different from what makes Sammy run. And: 'The most virulent Eve I've ever known was the production head of a major studio.'

The erasure of the differences between the sexes, which under other circumstances could be alarming, is in Mankiewicz's case and because it happens in the cinema a strategy for getting rid of sexually motivated prejudices and dissolving fixed lines of demarcation. It introduces movement, through the redistribution of images and sounds, into relations between the sexes.

What makes *The Ghost and Mrs Muir* so amusing, despite the yawning gulf at its centre, is the exchange of weapons. And the fact that it works successfully. Mrs Muir fights with a man's weapons, without for a moment abandoning her female identity. It is not so much that Mankiewicz wanted to make American cinema for adults, with more art or more ideas. He shows how, with invented and acted characters, one can defy the immutable fate of biology.

. . . .

In an old number of *Life* magazine, buried among advertisements of the day for lip pomade, practical stands for smoothing irons, denture fixatives and car-paint, there is a portrait of Mankiewicz, almost cubist in style, assembled from the views of fifteen people who knew the director well. As in many films of the day, a narrator provides the links. This is the new author, the reporter. To the interested reader of today, he embodies the age: what the 50s thought worth passing on in the description of a public figure. What lingers more than the observations of close friends and colleagues is the description, by big brother Herman, of the Mankiewicz family: a father preoccupied with studying and teaching, whose professorial pretensions spurred the ambitions of one son in particular and, as a way of showing his father what he was all about, triggered his Don Juanism. And then there was their mother: 'Joe spent most of his time with our mother. She was a round little woman who was uneducated in four languages. She spoke mangled German, mangled Russian, mangled Yiddish and mangled English. She raised Joe – Pop had no time for him.' What a seedbed for a career in Hollywood!

The identity crisis afflicting European authors around the turn of the century, possibly encouraged by the cinema, is not the same one that Mankiewicz had to fight in Hollywood. The *politique des auteurs*, invented by the French as a way to deal with American cinema, touches on the true *auteur* problem only indirectly. Above all it was a principle of selection which enabled people trapped in the traditional artistic categories to think about mass products. Mankiewicz pursues an American *politique des auteurs*, and it is a question not of original creations but of credits – which doesn't make the problem any less interesting, or any less in need of analysis.

'Here I am nearly halfway through life and what have I done?' sighs Mrs Muir. The cook, Martha, reminds her that she is still the mother of a daughter. One can't, Lucy says, take any credit for that. Then she sets about really doing something with what she has at her disposal. A work, even if it is one that is authenticated neither by name nor by person. Of course, the exchange between the two women is not to be found in the novel in this form.

A film author, by Mankiewicz's definition, is not the guarantor of the stylistic or artistic unity of a work. Authorship in Hollywood is a function defined and ensured by the credit, and whose culmination is the silver manikin called Oscar. Authorship is mobile and diverse. The camera and its gaze are not the only way of articulating an authorial perspective. Only the calculated mingling of formative elements originating in various media, each with its own relative autonomy, generates the tension that gives the film life. The director with authorial intentions who chooses actors as his substitutes to transfer what he has in mind to the screen is dependent on their abilities and appearance. He uses a delegation provided by the cinema. Originality belongs to the arts of the past. 'I became skilful at taking the colour of my environment without absorbing it, at participating in almost everything without becoming a part of anything.'

At the time of *The Ghost and Mrs Muir*, Mankiewicz was trying as best he could to play the part of the jobbing director. That wasn't enough for an *auteur* film. Some people say the film was just a piece of luck. But to achieve such anonymity, too many important names were involved in its realisation. Mankiewicz's personal achievement, which paradoxically drew on his experience as a producer that he hated so much, was the unique assembly of elements already shaped elsewhere. That determined the look of the film, and preserved its changing, glittering charms over the years.

The director's name, too long, too unpronounceable, too Central European for American tongues and ears, and which Mankiewicz ostentatiously maintained in the face of all the prevailing habits of abbreviating and adapting such names, nevertheless became the name of an *auteur* with the films he made after *The Ghost and Mrs Muir*.

CREDITS

·························

The Ghost and Mrs Muir

USA
1947
Production company
Twentieth Century-Fox
Film Corporation
US release
May 1947
Distributor (US)
Twentieth Century-Fox
UK release
30 June 1947
Distributor (UK)
Twentieth Century-Fox
Copyright date
13 June 1947
Producer
Fred Kohlmar
Director
Joseph L. Mankiewicz
Assistant director
Johnny Johnston
Screenplay
Philip Dunne from the
novel by R. A. Dick
(Josephine A. C. Leslie)
**Photography (black and
white)**
Charles Lang Jr
**Special photographic
effects**
Fred Sersen
Music
Bernard Herrmann
Editor
Dorothy Spencer
Art directors
Richard Day, George Davis
Set decorators
Thomas Little, Stewart
(Stuart) Reiss
Costumes
Eleanor Behm
**Costumes for Miss
Tierney designed by**
Oleg Cassini

Wardrobe director
Charles Le Maire
Make-up
Ben Nye
Sound
Bernard Freericks, Roger
Heman
104 mins

Gene Tierney
Lucy Muir
Rex Harrison
Captain Daniel Gregg
George Sanders
Miles Fairley
Edna Best
Martha Huggins
Vanessa Brown
Anna Muir, Lucy's daughter
Anna Lee
Mrs Miles Fairley
Robert Coote
Coombe Jr
Natalie Wood
Anna Muir as a child
Isobel Elsom
*Angelica Muir, Lucy's mother-
in-law*
Victoria Horne
Eva, Lucy's sister-in-law
Whitford Kane
Mr Sproule
Brad Slaven
Tacket & Sproule receptionist
Helen Freeman
Authoress
Dave Thursby
Scroggins
Stuart Holmes
Outraged train passenger
Heather Wilde
Fairley's maid
William Stelling
'Bill', Evelyn Anthony
Peregrine Scaithe
Rommie
Dog

New print produced by the
NFTVA from a nitrate
negative deposited by
Twentieth Century-Fox.

Available on VHS in the UK
on the FoxVideo label.

BIBLIOGRAPHY

· ·

Source material
Dick, R. A. *The Ghost and Mrs Muir* (London: 1972; New York: 1974).

Books about and with Mankiewicz
Carey, Gary. *More About 'All About Eve'* (New York: 1972).
Ciment, Michel. *Passeport pour Hollywood* (Paris: 1987).
Dick, Bernard F. *Joseph L. Mankiewicz* (New York: 1983).
Geist, Kenneth L. *People Will Talk* (New York: 1978).
Mérigeau, Pascal. *Mankiewicz* (Paris: 1993).

Interviews with Mankiewicz
Cahiers du cinéma, no. 178, May 1966.
Positif, no. 154, September 1973.

Articles about Mankiewicz
Coughlan, Robert. '15 Authors in Search of a Character Named Joseph L. Mankiewicz', *Life*, 12 March 1951.
Johnson, William. 'Heart of the Matter', *Film Comment*, May/June 1993.
Moullet, Luc. 'Mankiewicz: l'art de la machination', *Cahiers du cinéma*, no. 465, March 1993.
Narboni, Jean. 'Mankiewicz à la troisième personne', *Cahiers du cinéma*, no. 153, March 1964.
Rohmer, Eric. 'The Quiet American', *Cahiers du cinéma*, no. 86, August 1958.
E. S. 'L'Aventure de Mme Muir', *La Gazette du cinéma*, June 1950.

On Bernard Herrmann
Gilling, Ted. 'The Colour of the Music: an interview with Bernard Herrmann', *Sight and Sound*, vol. 41 no. 1, Winter 1971–2.
Smith, Stephen C. *A Heart at Fire's Centre* (Berkeley: University of California Press, 1991).

On Zanuck
Gussow, Mel. *Darryl F. Zanuck* (New York: 1971).

By Philip Dunne
Take Two (New York: 1980).

ALSO PUBLISHED

If you would like further information about future BFI Film Classics or about other books on film, media and popular culture from BFI Publishing, please write to:

BFI Film Classics
British Film Institute
21 Stephen Street
London
W1P 2LN